SPORTS
CHAMPIONSHIPS

THE WORLD SERIES

BY ALLAN MOREY

TORQUE ™

BELLWETHER MEDIA · MINNEAPOLIS, MN

TM

Are you ready to take it to the extreme? Torque books thrust you into the action-packed world of sports, vehicles, mystery, and adventure. These books may include dirt, smoke, fire, and chilling tales. **WARNING** : read at your own risk.

This edition first published in 2019 by Bellwether Media, Inc.

Library of Congress Cataloging-in-Publication Data

Names: Morey, Allan, author.
Title: The World Series / by Allan Morey.
Description: Minneapolis, Minnesota : Bellwether Media, Inc., 2019. | Series:
   Torque: Sports Championships | Includes bibliographical references and
   index. | Audience: Ages: 7-12. | Audience: Grades: 3 through 7.
Identifiers: LCCN 2018001833 (print) | LCCN 2018003258 (ebook) | ISBN
   9781626178687 (hardcover : alk. paper) | ISBN 9781681036090 (ebook) |
   ISBN 9781618914880 (paperback : alk. paper)
Subjects: LCSH: World Series (Baseball)–History–Juvenile literature. |
   Baseball–United States–History–Juvenile literature.
Classification: LCC GV878.4 (ebook) | LCC GV878.4 .M67 2019 (print) |
   DDC 796.357/46–dc23
LC record available at https://lccn.loc.gov/2018001833

Editor: Rebecca Sabelko   Designer: Jon Eppard

Printed in the United States of America, North Mankato, MN.

TABLE OF CONTENTS

BIG HITS

It is the final game of the 2017 World Series. The Houston Astros face the Los Angeles Dodgers.

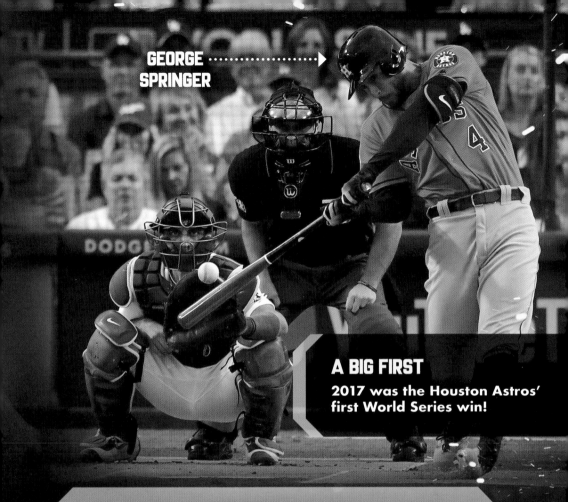

GEORGE SPRINGER

A BIG FIRST
2017 was the Houston Astros' first World Series win!

The Astros start strong. George Springer smacks a **double** to begin the game. His next at bat, he blasts a **home run**. After two **innings**, the Astros lead by five **runs**. They go on to win 5–1. They are World Series champs!

WHAT IS THE WORLD SERIES?

The World Series decides the Major **League** Baseball (MLB) champion. It is a best-of-seven series. The first team to win four games is the champ.

The MLB baseball season is 162 games long. The World Series is played at the end of the season. This series of games begins toward the end of October.

The winner of the World Series receives the Commissioner's Trophy. It was first awarded in 1967. It gets its name because the league's **commissioner** gives it to the winning team. The words "Presented by the Commissioner of Baseball" are stamped on the trophy.

There are also 30 flags on the trophy. Each flag stands for one team in the MLB.

COMMISSIONER'S ·········▶
TROPHY

2017
WORLD SERIES CHAMPS
HOUSTON ASTROS

HISTORY OF THE WORLD SERIES

In 1876, the National League of **Professional** Baseball Clubs (NL) was founded. Its creation makes baseball the oldest professional sport in North America! The American League (AL) was established in 1901.

1903 MLB GAME, BOSTON (AL) VS. CHICAGO (NL)

In 1903, the leagues joined to form the MLB. That year, the first World Series was played.

The Boston Americans (AL) beat the Pittsburgh Pirates (NL) in the 1903 World Series. It was a best-of-nine series. They won 5 games to 3.

The World Series has been played almost every year since 1903. In 1904, the two leagues had a disagreement. The World Series had to be canceled. A players' strike caused a cancellation in 1994.

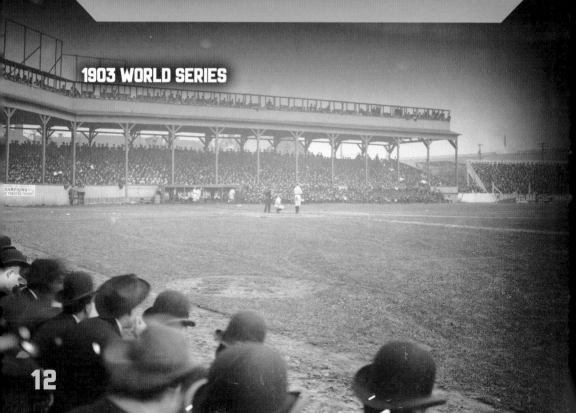

1903 WORLD SERIES

WORLD SERIES CHAMPS

THE NEW YORK YANKEES

1923, 1927, 1928, 1932, 1936, 1937, 1938, 1939,
1941, 1943, 1947, 1949, 1950, 1951, 1952, 1953,
1956, 1958, 1961, 1962, 1977, 1978, 1996, 1998,
1999, 2000, 2009

WORLD SERIES MVP

Yogi Berra played for the Yankees from 1946 to
1963 and in 1965. He helped them win 10 World
Series. He has been a World Series champ more
than any other MLB player!

YOGI BERRA

ROAD TO THE WORLD SERIES

The NL and AL both have 15 teams. Each league is divided into three **divisions** of 5 teams.

Each league has 5 teams that make it to the **playoffs**. This includes 3 division winners and 2 **wild card** teams. Wild card spots go to the teams with the next best records after the division winners.

The first playoff game is the wild card round. The winner and 3 division winners then play in the Division Series. This is a five-game series.

The 2 remaining teams in each division move on to the League Championship Series. This is a seven-game series. The NL and AL winners of the League Championship Series meet in the World Series.

MLB PLAYOFF BRACKET

AMERICAN LEAGUE

WILD CARD ROUND

DIVISION SERIES

LEAGUE CHAMPIONSHIP SERIES

WORLD SERIES

SEEDING

MLB playoff teams are seeded, or ranked, from one to five. Teams with the highest seed get home-field advantage. The first, second, and last games of each series are played at their fields.

**MLB
CHAMPION**

**NATIONAL
LEAGUE**

WORLD SERIES

**LEAGUE
CHAMPIONSHIP
SERIES**

**DIVISION
SERIES**

**WILD CARD
ROUND**

FIRST PITCH

Well-known people often throw the first pitch of a baseball game. Everyone from presidents to pop stars have done this for World Series games. During Game 7 in 2017, baseball greats Sandy Koufax and Don Newcombe threw out the first pitch together.

Watching the first pitch is just the beginning of the excitement during the World Series!

GLOSSARY

commissioner—an official in charge of overseeing a professional sport league

divisions—small groupings of sports teams; there are usually several divisions of teams in a league.

double—a hit that allows a batter to get to second base

home run—a hit that allows a batter to go around all four bases and score a run

innings—parts of a baseball game during which each team gets to bat until they have three outs; baseball games have nine innings.

league—a large grouping of sports teams that often play each other

playoffs—games played after the regular season is over; playoff games determine which teams play in the World Series.

professional—related to a player or team that makes money playing a sport

runs—points in a baseball game

wild card—a team selected to fill in the final spots of a playoff tournament

TO LEARN MORE

AT THE LIBRARY

Braun, Eric. *Baseball Is a Numbers Game: A Fan's Guide to Stats*. North Mankato, Minn.: Capstone Press, 2018.

Mikoley, Kate. *Baseball: Stats, Facts, and Figures*. New York, N.Y.: Gareth Stevens Publishing, 2018.

Morey, Allan. *Baseball Records*. Minneapolis, Minn.: Bellwether Media, 2018.

ON THE WEB

Learning more about the World Series is as easy as 1, 2, 3.

1. Go to www.factsurfer.com.

2. Enter "World Series" into the search box.

3. Click the "Surf" button and you will see a list of related web sites.

With factsurfer.com, finding more information is just a click away.

INDEX